∾ SACRED CELTIC PLACES

SACRED CELTIC PLACES

Iain Zaczek

Photography by
David Lyons

COLLINS & BROWN

First published in Great Britain in 2002 by
Collins & Brown Limited
64 Brewery Road, London N7 9NT

A member of **Chrysalis** Books plc

1 2 3 4 5 6 7 8 9

British Library Cataloguing-in-Publication Data:
A catalogue record for this title is available from the
British Library.

ISBN 1 85585 986 6

Conceived, edited and designed by
Collins & Brown Limited

Designed by Liz Brown

Printed in Hong Kong

FRONT COVER: Callanish Standing Stones, Lewis
SPINE: Kells Cross, County Meath
BACK COVER: (left to right) Dunnottar Castle,
Kincardine; Passage Tomb, Newgrange; Dun Aenghus
fort, Aran Islands; Glendalough monastery, County
Wicklow
FRONTISPIECE: Eilean Donan castle, Ross & Cromarty
CONTENTS: Glencoe, Argyll

Contents

INTRODUCTION

Ring of Brodgar
page 38
Once consisting
of sixty slabs
surrounded by a
ditch, this is
Scotland's largest
peninsula.

IN THE FAR WESTERN REACHES OF Europe, the Celts were a dominant force for centuries until the arrival of the Normans brought them into line with continental developments. During this period of comparative isolation, they developed a culture that was both mysterious and elusive. Their literature was oral, rather than written; their religious practices were veiled in secrecy; and their art was non-descriptive, consisting mainly of stylized figures or hypnotic, abstract designs. In spite of this, the Celtic spirit became deeply embedded in the West, leaving a permanent mark on the landscapes of Scotland, Ireland and Wales.

The emphasis on land is significant, for the Celts were essentially a tribal people and the fortunes of the land were of relevance to all. Most of their deities, although sometimes fictionalized as warriors or lovers, were actually nature gods. This is made clear not only from legends, but also from a wealth of archaeological evidence. Water, in particular, was greatly revered. There were popular cults for many river goddesses, such as Bóann (the Boyne), Sinann (the Shannon) and Sabrina (the Severn), and precious objects were frequently deposited at these and other watery sites, as a form of sacrifice. Similarly, Celtic kings took part in sacred rituals, which linked the fertility of their lands with the strength of their rule (see page 52).

Even in the Christian era, the bounty of nature was appreciated. Monks and anchorites invariably chose to live in remote spots far from the bustle of humanity, and it is no accident that some of these early clerics gained a reputation for their verses, which extolled the beauty of nature, while citing it as a proof of God's love for His flock.

Unlike the feudal system, where land was parcelled out with great precision, the Celtic tribes held much of their land in common. At root, their society was bound together by family ties. In Ireland, the main territorial unit was the *tuath* ('tribe' or 'people'), which was large enough to produce a force of anything between 500 and 3,000 warriors. Within each *tuath*, the practice of fostering children out was used extensively, to create closer bonds between

The Blasket Islands
page 80
Because of their remote location, lying off the tip of the Dingle peninsula, these rocky isles became a rich storehouse of ancient folklore.

individual families. In Scotland, the clan system operated along similar lines.

By organizing themselves around the extended family, the Celts achieved great personal loyalty and considerable social cohesion at a local level. In the grander scheme of things, though, the system had some major disadvantages. Feuding was endemic, and the Celts were always vulnerable to enemies, who could achieve unity on a larger scale. In this context, the term 'king' may be misleading. Ireland had several layers of kingship and, at its lowest level, this signified nothing more than a tribal chieftain.

For most of the Celtic period, real power was vested in the kings of the five provinces. These ancient divisions consisted of four familiar names – Munster, Ulster, Leinster and Connaught – together with *Mide* or 'the Middle Kingdom'. Mide coincided roughly with the modern counties of Meath and Westmeath. Despite its modest size, it held great prestige, because it contained Tara – the seat of the high kings. This imposing title meant more in symbolic terms than in actual power. For although, in theory, the high king enjoyed supremacy over all other Irish rulers, this was never a political reality. Only one high king came close to fulfilling the goal of national leadership and that was Brian Boru (d. 1014). This Munster leader achieved the same

sort of status as Wallace and Bruce in Scotland, especially after his victory over the Vikings at the Battle of Clontarf (1014).

The Scots themselves emerged out of the tribal squabbles in Ireland. The Scotti were a Gaelic people, living in the north-east. There was considerable competition for territory in this part of Ulster, however, so one branch of the tribe – the Dál Riata – decided to migrate to Argyll in *c.* 500 AD. There, they founded the tiny kingdom of Dalriada, choosing Dunadd (see pages 60–1) as their principal stronghold. The Dál Riata were only separated from their original homeland in Antrim by a very narrow stretch of water (about twelve miles), so close contacts were maintained with other members of the tribe. Indeed, for more than a century, the kingdom of Dalriada included territory in both Argyll and Ulster.

After deciding to make their future in Argyll, the Scots' chief rivals were the Picts. The latter were also a Celtic people and had been resident in Britain since perhaps as early as the sixth century BC. After centuries of bitter enmity, the two tribes merged to create the kingdom of Alba (*c.* 843), which, in turn, formed the basis of the Scottish nation.

Navan Fort
page 61
This is the fabled site of Emain Macha, where Conchobar built a glittering palace and ruled over the people of Ulster.

ANCESTORS

When the Celts arrived in the West, they found the monuments of other, prehistoric peoples scattered throughout the land. Ranging from imposing stone circles and forts, to massive tombs decorated with mysterious carvings, these relics from a bygone age made a deep impression upon the newcomers. Wherever possible, they tried to use the structures, turning them into farmsteads or military strongholds. In other cases, where the original function of the monument was less obvious, they revered them, weaving them into the fabric of their own culture.

What did the Celts think of their predecessors? We cannot know for certain. It is clear, nonetheless, that they respected them enough to leave most of their monuments intact. By and large, they did not pull down standing stones and megalithic tombs simply to use them as building material. Instead, they gave them a place in their legends, thus absorbing them into their own, distinctive vision of the past.

Dun Aenghus
Aran Islands, County Galway
The Celts ascribed the construction of this magnificent cliff-top fort to the Fir Bolg, an ancient, mythical tribe, whom some sources have linked with the Belgae.

Migration of the Celts

THE CELTS DID NOT ORIGINATE IN the West. As far as historians can tell, they surfaced in central Europe in around the sixth century BC, gradually migrating westwards over the following centuries. Then, as the Roman Empire expanded, the Celts were pushed towards the fringes of Europe. By the first century BC, they had been penned back into some of the remotest corners of the continent – Scotland, Ireland, Wales, Cornwall and Brittany.

As they settled in these distant outposts, the Celts inevitably became aware of the achievements of their forerunners. The magnificent complex of tombs on the Boyne, for example – Newgrange, Dowth, Knowth – was considerably grander than most of the Celts' own structures. With this in mind, the newcomers had to adapt the legacy of the past, either using or reinventing it to suit their own ends.

Re-use of buildings

There is no doubt that the Celts made extensive use of many sites created by their predecessors. Domestic buildings and farmsteads were simply reoccupied, with suitable alterations and additions over the years. At Jarlshof for instance (page 24), there is concrete proof that the place was inhabited by many different groups of settlers, from the Bronze Age right through to Viking times. This process is most clearly seen in the Orkney and Shetland Isles, where the relative inaccessibility of the sites has preserved the evidence, but the same practices were undoubtedly in operation throughout other Celtic territories.

History and legend

By contrast, theories about the Celtic reinvention of the past are far more controversial. The main problem, in this respect, is that the Celts did not write down literary or historical matter. Instead, they transmitted it orally, from generation to generation. As a result, much information was lost or distorted over the centuries. There is no known Celtic creation myth, for example, perhaps because Christian scribes were unwilling to record it. Even so, a considerable body of material did survive in Ireland, much of it apparently dating back to the Iron Age. Most of this deals with legends, but there are two important texts, which relate to Ireland's past. These are the *Book of Invasions* and the *Cycle of the Kings*.

The oldest version of the *Book of Invasions* only dates from the twelfth century, but it contains material that is much older. As the title suggests, the narrative describes the waves of early settlers, who occupied Ireland prior to the arrival of the Celts. Inevitably, historians have examined it closely, hoping to ascertain if any of the incursions are based on historical reality.

The *Book of Invasions* lists seven distinct phases of occupation. In chronological order, the invaders were Cesair and her companions, the Partholonians, the

Nemedians, the Fomorians, the Fir Bolg, the Tuatha Dé Danaan and the Milesians. Some of these were clearly invented by later Christian commentators. Cesair, for example, was cited as the granddaughter of Noah. Most of the others, though, have been linked with genuine tribes. The Milesians, for instance, have often been seen as a fictionalized equivalent of the Gaels. One of their leaders, a woman named Scota, was cited as the ancestor of the Scotti, while Ith, the first Milesian to land on Irish soil, was killed on a spying mission at the great fortress of Aileach (page 54).

Raiders and invasions

Where links with specific sites are concerned, the most significant 'invaders' were the Tuatha Dé Danaan, the Fomorians and the Fir Bolg. The Danaan became identified with the Irish gods, and will be discussed in the following chapter (see pages 34–5). The Fomorians were also initially regarded as deities, albeit malevolent ones, but later versions of the text describe them as pirates. As such, they may well be associated with the Norse and Danish raiders, who pillaged the Irish coast. The Fomorians' chief base was on Tory Island (page 40), but they also participated in battles at Cnámross (now Camross, County Laois) and Mag Tuired (page 48; now Moytura, County Sligo).

The Fir Bolg have been linked with a number of early Celtic tribes, most notably the Laigin (the founders of

Leinster), the Erainn and the Belgae (the Gaulish people who eventually gave their name to Belgium). After their defeat by the Tuatha Dé Danaan, the Fir Bolg were scattered to the remotest corners of Ireland, which explains their frequent association with islands and coastal regions. There, they gained a formidable reputation as builders, being hailed as the creators of some of Ireland's most spectacular forts (pages 10 and 22).

Fourknocks, County Meath
The scribings found at this and other passage tombs were later incorporated into traditional, Celtic design.

౷ Passage Tomb

NEWGRANGE **COUNTY MEATH**

The ancient Celts were so impressed with the megalithic monuments at Newgrange that they linked them with their own gods. In Irish legend, it was cited as the palace of the Dagda, the father of the gods, although at a later stage, he was supplanted by Oenghus, the god of love, who managed to trick him into leaving the place. Because of these associations, Newgrange was usually described as a house of plenty, with trees that were always in fruit and cooking pots that were never empty.

The elaborate spiral designs on the kerbstone and the interior walls of Newgrange are often thought to be typically Celtic, but in fact they predate the arrival of the Celts. Historians have suggested that the spirals had a symbolic meaning for the builders of the tomb, representing the movement of the sun. This is quite feasible, since the alignment of the monument clearly served an astronomical function. At the winter solstice, a shaft of sunlight penetrates the full length of the passage and casts light on the carvings.

⊚⊚ Lough Gur

COUNTY LIMERICK

The wide and varied selection of prehistoric remains around Lough Gur indicates that it has always been an area of great spiritual significance. Among other things, there is a stone circle, a crannog and a Neolithic burial place. Conscious of this, the Celts linked it with the

Otherworld. More specifically, they believed that it was one of the entrances to Tir na nOg. This was the fabled Land of Youth, where there was no sickness or old age. Ossian spent 300 years there, thinking he had only been away from home for a single day.

In a later legend, Gerald, Earl of Desmond, vanished in this place. Some say that he turned into a goldfinch; others that he went to live in a castle at the bottom of Lough Gur, reappearing once every seven years.

⊚⊚ Loughcrew

COUNTY MEATH

Loughcrew is an extensive prehistoric cemetery, containing more than thirty chambered cairns. From early times, the Celts believed that the largest of these, Cairn 'T', was the grave of Ollamh Fódla, one of their ancient kings. During his rule at Tara, he was said to have become Ireland's first law-giver and to have been responsible for dividing the country into its five, original kingdoms.

Loughcrew's cemetery, from which this picture was taken, spreads over the *Sliab na Caillighe* ('the Mountain of the Hag'), which has long been seen as a reference to the sorceress who turned the youthful Finn MacCool into an old man.

◎◎ Achill Island

COUNTY MAYO

Lying to the north of Clew Bay, Achill Island was long regarded as a place of immense antiquity. The ancient Celts spoke of a Hawk of Achill, which was said to have lived for thousands of years. In a colourful tale, the bird exchanged reminiscences with Fintan mac Bóchra, an aged seer. Fintan boasted how he had escaped the biblical flood by becoming a one-eyed salmon, an eagle and then a hawk, before returning to his human form. In reply, the hawk remarked that it had witnessed the exploits of Cú Chulainn and the coming of Christianity.

◎◎ Poulnabrone

THE BURREN **COUNTY CLARE**

Set on a rocky, limestone plateau, this is one of Ireland's most impressive examples of a dolmen. Pre-Celtic people used structures of this kind as elaborate burial chambers but, impressed by their dramatic design, the Celts often interpreted them in other, more fanciful ways. In many cases, they likened them to the furniture or playthings of giants. This notion was given added weight by the fact that, in some instances, the Celts regarded their gods as an ancient race of giants. One legend, in particular, was linked with dolmens. The story of Diarmaid and Gráinne (see pages 84–5) invited the comparison, because so much of the narrative took place in the open countryside. As a result, many dolmens became known as the 'bower' or the 'beds' of this pair.

Because of their resemblance to tables (the literal meaning of dolmen is 'table-stone'), there was also a popular view that these tombs had been altars. It was said that the druids had performed human sacrifices upon them.

෧෨ Clew Bay

COUNTY MAYO

Situated to the north of Croagh Patrick, Ireland's holy mountain, Clew Bay features in the creation myths of both the Fir Bolg and the province of Connacht. In the pseudo-historical text of the *Book of Invasions*, it was related how the Fir Bolg fled to the distant parts of the north-west, after they were defeated by the Tuatha Dé Danaan and expelled from the rest of Ireland. A warrior named Sreng, however, was offered the region as a peace settlement, after he had severed the arm of a Danaan king, and he went on to become the ancestor of the Connacht rulers.

෧෨ Creevykeel

COUNTY SLIGO

The prehistoric tombs at the edge of this hamlet have long been known as the Giants' Graves. In many parts of the country, monuments of this kind would have been ascribed to a particular deity, since the Irish gods were frequently portrayed as giants. In this instance, however, there is no association with a specific god; the locals were simply impressed by the unusual size and complexity of the ancient tombs.

Creevykeel boasts one of the finest examples of a court cairn. This type of grave was normally distinguished by an elongated cairn and a semicircular forecourt, shaped like a claw, at the entrance to the chamber. The version at Creevykeel was remarkably large, extending for almost seventy yards, and its paved court was located within the mound. Archaeologists have speculated that court cairns were not so much graves as temples, and that some ritual took place in the court area. If so, then Creevykeel clearly possessed a high degree of sanctity, which may have lingered in the memory of local inhabitants.

∞ Dun Duchathair

INISHMORE **ARAN ISLANDS**

There are no historical records relating to the origins of the magnificent promontory forts on the Aran Islands, and historians cannot agree on their date. The *Book of Invasions*, however, declared that they were built by the Fir Bolg, who were exiled here following their defeat at the Battle of Mag Tuired. Their owners were not identified, with the exception of Dun Aenghus (page 10), which was built for a chieftain called Angus, the supposed ancestor of the Déisi tribe. The name of Dun Duchathair, however, offers no such clues, as it simply means 'Dark Fort'.

∞ Knap of Howar

PAPA WESTRAY **ORKNEY**

The Knap of Howar ('knoll of mounds') can lay claim to being Scotland's oldest homestead, dating back to *c.* 3400 BC. The two Neolithic structures were built inside an earlier midden, one providing living quarters for the inhabitants, the other serving as a combined storeroom and workshop. The houses do not appear to have been disturbed during the Celtic period, when the island became a pilgrimage centre, dedicated to the cult of St Tredwell. She suffered at the hands of a Pictish king, but her shrine was said to possess curative powers for eye complaints.

◎ Jarlshof

SHETLAND

More than any other prehistoric site, Jarlshof offers a sense of the continuity which existed between different generations and cultures in this remote region. For traces of at least five different phases of construction can be found, ranging from the Bronze Age to the seventeenth century. From the Bronze Age, there are huts and cattle stalls. Iron Age dwellers added a broch and Pictish wheel-houses, while the Vikings erected longhouses in the ninth century. During the Middle Ages, the place became a rambling farmstead before, in the sixteenth century, Robert Stewart, Earl of Orkney, began work on the impressive laird's house, which was later extended by his son.

Jarlshof's name might suggest that the main period of activity occurred during Viking times, but this is misleading. In fact, the name is a pure invention, coined by Sir Walter Scott when he chose this place as the setting for his novel, *The Pirate* (1821).

∞ Broch of Gurness

ORKNEY

Brochs were circular, drystone towers, used principally for defence but also sheltering a series of smaller, domestic homesteads within their walls. They were unique to Scotland although, superficially at least, they bear some resemblance to Irish ring-forts and cashels. The Gurness settlement was established during the Iron Age, but was later inhabited by both Picts and Vikings. The former, for example, left behind a symbol-stone, an iron knife with an ogham inscription and various brooch-moulds, while the principal Viking find was a woman's tomb, containing jewellery and domestic implements.

෧ Skara Brae

ORKNEY

This is arguably Scotland's most important prehistoric site; a Neolithic village which remained concealed from the outside world for centuries until, in 1850, a violent storm blew away the layers of sand which had covered it. Underneath, there were eight houses, which had been occupied from *c*. 3100 to 2500 BC. Normally, later generations would have re-used these buildings, so it is likely that entire site had been submerged. This may have been the result of a natural disaster, or the settlement may have been deliberately filled in, for ritual reasons.

The village is virtually subterranean, a honeycomb of tiny dwelling-places linked by narrow passages. The houses themselves, however, are less interesting than the varied array of domestic items that were uncovered. These include stone beds, larder-pools for fish, a hearth, a dresser and various types of cupboard, together with smaller finds, such as pottery, beads and tools.

෧ Clickhimin

LERWICK **SHETLAND**

The most striking part of this complex site is its massive broch, although other parts of the settlement are far older, dating back to *c*. 700 BC. Initially, the community was centred around a plain farmstead, to which a wheel-house (a circular, partitioned building) was later added. The place was certainly not isolated, for excavations have revealed foreign imports among the ruins. The most intriguing of these is a Roman-style, glass bowl, which was apparently produced at Alexandria in *c*. 100 AD.

Duncansby Head

CAITHNESS

These treacherous rocks, known as the Stacks of Duncansby, are located at the north-eastern tip of Scotland, just a couple of miles away from John O'Groats. Duncansby itself became an important base for the Earls of Caithness. Its coastal position was highly convenient, since these lords were also often the rulers of Orkney.

For the most part, Duncansby played a greater part in Scandinavian, rather than Celtic history. There were times, however, when these two spheres of influence overlapped, most notably during the reign of Macbeth. For this celebrated Scottish king was the half-brother of Thorfinn the Mighty and, throughout their respective reigns, the two men offered each other mutual assistance. Thorfinn had been installed at Duncansby as the Earl of Caithness by Malcolm II, but he later assisted Macbeth in wresting the throne from Duncan. In return, Macbeth turned a blind eye when Thorfinn carried out raids on western Scotland and the Isle of Man.

Fortingall

PERTHSHIRE

The richness of Fortingall's prehistoric remains bear witness to its antiquity. Among other things, they include stone circles, an Iron Age ring-fort and various cup-marked stones. More dubious, however, is the old tradition that this was the birthplace of Pontius Pilate. His father, so the story goes, was an envoy sent from Rome, while his mother was a member of the Menzies clan. In further 'confirmation' of this tale, some local earthworks have been dubbed the 'Praetorium', although they are probably just the vestiges of a medieval homestead.

GODS

The Celts respected the sanctity of the many ritual sites which earlier generations had left behind. For the most part, they continued to regard them as holy places, describing them as the palaces or temples of their own deities. These gods were known as the Tuatha Dé Danaan, a shadowy race of divine beings who, according to legend, ruled Ireland for almost three hundred years, before being supplanted by invading Celtic warriors.

The details of the Celts' religious practices are far from clear, largely because of the cloak of secrecy employed by the druids. This caste of priest-like officials organized their holy rituals for centuries, but few traces of their mysterious craft have been preserved, apart from a series of ogham inscriptions. This did not prevent later generations from inventing their own notions about the druids, however, portraying them as little more than wizards.

Standing Stones – Callanish, Lewis
The cruciform arrangement of the stones
is linked with sun-worship. There is also a
'druidical circle' which, according to legend,
was formed by the petrified remains of
sacrificial victims.

Ancient divinities

THE IRISH PANTHEON OF GODS was uniquely bound up with its landscape. According to legend, it sprang from a divine race of beings, known as the Tuatha Dé Danaan. The literal meaning of this was 'People of the Goddess Danu', referring to the matriarchal deity worshipped by the Celts of continental Europe. Her name is most famously preserved in the River Danube.

In the *Book of Invasions*, the Tuatha Dé Danaan were defined as a race of gods who invaded Ireland, seizing power from the Fir Bolg. Their divine origins were emphasized by the fact that they were borne to Ireland on a dark, thunderous cloud, rather than on a fleet of ships. The Danaans then ruled for 297 years before they, in turn, were ousted from power by the Milesians, the human ancestors of the Celts.

Inhabitants of the underworld

After their defeat, the Tuatha Dé Danaan were not forced out of Ireland. Instead, they were driven underground, where they came to inhabit the Otherworld. This supernatural realm was, in many ways, a parallel universe, where daily life continued much as before, but without the threat of sickness, old age or death. In the Otherworld, the gods dwelt in *sídhe* or 'fairy mounds'. Below the earth, these *sídhe* were sumptuous palaces, where the Danaans could feast, drink and live a life of ease. Above the ground, they were visible to humans as mounds or hills. In particular, they were linked with the great cairns and burial mounds that had been constructed in prehistoric times.

Landscape and the gods

In this way, the Celtic landscape became littered with memorials to the ancient gods. The most celebrated example was Newgrange (pages 14–5), which was seen as the home of both the Dagda and his son, the love-god Oenghus, but the same pattern was repeated at many other megalithic sites. The Hill of Allen in County Kildare, for instance, was traditionally viewed as the

Dunloe, County Kerry
These markings are examples of ogham, a rudimentary form of writing employed by the Druids. It appears to have had ritual or magical overtones.

ancient palace of Nuadu of the Silver Arm, which later passed to Finn MacCool.

The reality of the Celts' own religious practices is almost as mysterious as the fairy realm of their gods. For, due to the secretive ways of the druids, virtually no details of their rites have survived. Even so, it is clear that the druids held an important and wide-ranging role in Celtic society. In addition to supervising a variety of sacrifices and rituals, they were expected to act as judges, royal advisers and guardians of tribal knowledge. This knowledge was regarded as so sacred that it could never be written down. Instead, it was transmitted orally, from one generation of druids to the next.

Ogham inscriptions

Some things were written down, however, and these were preserved in a very basic form of script, known as ogham. In this, individual letters of the alphabet were conveyed by a series of straight or slanting lines. Apparently, these were usually notched onto pieces of bark, although no examples of this fragile medium have survived. Instead, the only existing ogham inscriptions are those preserved on large stones or pillars (see page 48, for example). The precise function of these ogham stones has been the subject of much debate. Among other things, they have been interpreted as memorials to the dead, boundary markers or ritual stones. They are mainly associated with southern Ireland – particularly,

Boa Island, County Fermanagh
With its powerful, stylized features, this carving is typical of the way the ancient Celts portrayed their gods.

Kerry and Cork – but they were also used in other Celtic territories. Examples have been found in Scotland, Wales, Cornwall and the Isle of Man.

Whatever their original purpose, ogham stones provide the only tangible reminders of druidic activity in the Celtic landscape. Nevertheless, this did not prevent later commentators from presenting a very different picture. During the Romantic era, when there was a huge revival of interest in the Celts, historians believed that the druids had been responsible for creating some of the most impressive, prehistoric monuments. Accordingly, many stone circles were interpreted as druid temples, while dolmens were regarded as massive altars, where gory sacrifices were carried out.

⊚⊚ The Turoe Stone

COUNTY GALWAY

Comparatively little is known about the religious practices of the prehistoric Celts, but this massive, decorated stone gives some impression of their complexity. Almost certainly, it was designed for some ritual purpose, though its precise symbolism remains unclear. Some historians have noted its similarity to the Navel Stone at Delphi, arguing that it was a focus for the same sort of divination rites. More commonly, though, its phallic shape has suggested a link with fertility. This theory is strengthened by the fact that the Turoe Stone was originally sited in a ring-fort known as the Rath of Feerwore ('Rath of the Strong Men').

⊚⊚ Fair Head

COUNTY ANTRIM

Fair Head is known for its geological formations. This image shows a small lake on the top with a prehistoric man-made island and crannog. The most notable formation of Fair Head, however, is *Carraig Uisneach* ('Rock of Uisneach'). This commemorates a famous love story from Irish legend, in which Deirdre and Naoise eloped to Scotland. Eventually, however, they were lured back to Ulster, where Naoise was slain by a jealous suitor. In its original form, this tale would have been a divine romance, for Naoise's father was Uisneach, who, in turn, was related to the love-god, Oenghus.

∾ Ring of Brodgar

NEAR STENNESS **ORKNEY**

In the Orkneys, there was a longstanding tradition that this famous stone circle was designed for the worship of the sun. Writing in 1703, Martin Martin described the Ring of Brodgar and the neighbouring circle at Stenness as ancient temples to the sun and moon. Archaeological evidence has lent support to this view, for a number of prehistoric axe-heads were buried at Brodgar. Axes were viewed as symbols of thunderbolts and, because they could create sparks of fire, were also linked with solar cults. In Celtic legend, they were associated with the sky-god Taranis, whose name means 'the Thunderer'.

෨ Tory Island

COUNTY DONEGAL

In Irish legend, islands were frequently regarded as mysterious, otherworldly places. Tory Island, for example, was seen as the home of the Fomorians, a race of evil deities. Originally, they were visualized as giant demons, often suffering from grotesque, physical deformities, but in the historic period they came to be viewed as merciless sea-raiders.

The leader of the Fomorians was Balor of the Baleful Eye, so-called because his single eye brought death to anyone who gazed on it. On Tory Island, his name is still preserved in the ruined stronghold of *Dun Bhalair* ('Balor's Fort'). Here, it is said, Balor imprisoned his daughter, after hearing a prophecy that he would be slain by his grandson. He could not cheat his fate, however, and was eventually bested by Lugh, who blinded him with a slingshot. Since the latter was a sun-god, this contest has sometimes been seen as a symbol of the New Year (Lugh) supplanting the Old Year (Balor).

෨ Boa Island

COUNTY FERMANAGH

This carved figure is situated in an area where pagan influences remained strong, long after Christianity had taken root. The island was an important centre of druid activity. There was also a cult devoted to Badb, from which the word 'Boa' is derived. Badb was an Irish war-goddess, who frequently took on the form of a hooded crow. She also appeared on battlefields, inciting soldiers to fight, or as the ghostly 'washer at the ford', cleaning the armour of warriors who were about to die.

◎ Maeve's Cairn

CARROWMORE **COUNTY SLIGO**

In Ireland, the Celts loved to endow prehistoric sites with mythological connotations. With its extensive megalithic cemetery, its ring-forts and its pillar-stones, Carrowmore (part of which is shown here in the foreground) was clearly a very holy place in ancient times and, as a result, it became linked with one of the most powerful deities of all. Medb, or Maeve, was a goddess of war and sovereignty. The tomb named after her can be seen on top of the hill in the distance. As the goddess of sovereignty, she played an important role in the kingship rites at Tara. As part of their inauguration ceremony, new kings entered into a ritual union with Maeve. This procedure appears to have included sacred libations, for the literal meaning of the goddess's name is 'she who intoxicates'. The drink 'mead', stems from the same root.

In Irish legend, Maeve was also portrayed as the warrior-queen of Connacht. As such, she figured prominently in the famous epic, *The Cattle Raid of Cooley*. It was she who stole the magical bull, which triggered off a war with Ulster and provoked her long-running feud with Cú Chulainn.

෯ Sheela-na-gig

KILLINABOY **COUNTY CLARE**

Mystery surrounds the precise origin of this curious type of carving, although it is generally thought to represent a Celtic goddess of fertility. Sheela-na-gigs were often placed on the walls of Irish castles and churches, with the apparent intention of warding off evil. Later generations were sometimes shocked by the blatant sexuality of the image, although this concern was clearly not shared by early patrons. One such carving, for example, can be found on the side of a bishop's tomb!

෯ Sligo Bay

COUNTY SLIGO

This is Maeve's realm, pictured from the site of her supposed burial place. In the legends, she is portrayed as part-goddess, part-queen. She meddles in human affairs, making war against Ulster and, in particular, against Cú Chulainn, her implacable foe. At the same time, she has supernatural powers. She can shape-shift, she can run with the speed of a horse, and her mere presence can drain mortals of their life-force. Maeve used these magical powers to lure Cú Chulainn to his death, but could not save herself from her own, bizarre demise. She was eventually slain by a lump of stale cheese, fired as a slingshot.

❧ Drombeg Stone Circle

COUNTY CORK

Drombeg is one of the finest recumbent stone circles in Ireland. These usually featured one large, horizontal stone, situated directly opposite tall portal stones, at the far side of the ring. It has been suggested that this arrangement was designed to facilitate astronomical alignments, thus strengthening the argument that this type of circle was linked with solar or lunar worship. Within the Celtic period there was a ritual burial at Drombeg. Cremated bones were placed in a pot, which was deliberately broken, before being interred in the centre of the ring. There is also evidence that devotees either danced or processed around the portal stones.

⊚⊚ Ogham Stone

DUNLOE **COUNTY KERRY**

Traditionally, ogham was invented by Ogma, the Irish god of literature and eloquence. His skill with words earned him the nickname *Cermait* ('honey-mouthed'). Despite this, Ogma featured principally as a warrior in the early legends. He was one of the three great champions of the Tuatha Dé Danaan, distinguishing himself at the battle of Mag Tuired, where he slew Indech the Fomorian. Ogma can probably be identified with Ogmios, the Gaulish god of rhetoric. Like his Irish counterpart, the latter was famed for his strength and eloquence.

⊚⊚ Cup-and-Ring Marks

BALUACRAIG, KILMARTEN VALLEY **ARGYLL**

These enigmatic, Bronze-Age markings can be found throughout the Celtic world. Their purpose is uncertain, although they are usually interpreted as evidence of a solar cult. On certain megalithic monuments, they seem designed to catch the sunlight at solstice time, as if to encourage its life-giving activities. Alternatively, they have been viewed as primitive sundials, as maps to sacred sites, or even simply as gaming boards.

ROYAL SITES

Throughout the ancient Celtic world, kingship was regarded as a religious office, as much as a secular one. This was reflected in the immense complexity of the inauguration rites, as well as the unusual nature of some royal sites. In several cases, these were associated with ancient monuments, which had served entirely different purposes in prehistoric times. Similarly in the legends, there was also often a blurring of the distinction between royalty and divinity, with the result that many mythological rulers were endowed with supernatural powers.

Even in the context of later, secular history, royalty remained a complicated issue. In Ireland, there were several layers of kingship, ranging from the regional kings, who were often little more than tribal chiefs, to the largely symbolic role of the high king. In Scotland, the title grew in importance, as the realm expanded from the tiny kingdom of Dalriada to the modern, Scottish nation. It was also applied to the Jacobite leaders, who were never recognized in England, but were true kings in the eyes of Highlanders.

Hill of Ushnagh
County Westmeath
Long revered as the mystical heart of
Ireland, Ushnagh is said to have been the
stronghold of Tuathal Teachtmhair, one of
the earliest high kings (second century AD?).

Kingship and religion

FROM ANCIENT TIMES, THE ROLES of kingship and religion were closely intertwined in Celtic society. Every king claimed divine ancestry and, as part of his inauguration ceremony, he was expected to take part in a ritual mating with one of the goddesses of sovereignty. The latter symbolized the fortunes of the land, for the Celts believed that there was a direct correlation between the performance of a monarch and the prosperity of his domain. If a king ruled well, then the fertility of the land was assured; if not, then its crops would suffer.

In Ireland, the most sacred rites took place at Tara (pages 56–7), where the goddess in question was Maeve. Tara was particularly important, because it was the seat of the high king. The latter's religious significance was emphasized by the elaborate nature of the *tarbhfhess*, the ritual which led to his selection. In this mystical ceremony, a man was given a strange broth – a type of sleeping potion, which included morsels of bull-flesh. Then, while he slept, four druids chanted an 'incantation of truth' over the man, who was expected to receive a vision, in which the identity of the new king would be revealed. The successful candidate also had to undergo a number of other initiation tests. Most famously, he had to place his hands on the *Lia Fáil*, an ancient stone which gave out a piercing scream when touched by the rightful king.

Tara and Ushnagh

The choice of Tara as Ireland's principal royal seat underlines the links between religion and kingship. The original, prehistoric site contained an assortment of tombs, burial mounds, earthworks and forts but, even in its earliest stages, it was never a powerful stronghold. Instead, its importance lay in its position. The literal meaning of Tara is 'place with a view', which indicates that – in common with the nearby Hill of Ushnagh (page

50) – landmarks from all five of the ancient provinces could be seen from its summit. As a result, Tara and Ushnagh were regarded as the twin hearts of Ireland, and became the focal points of major 'royal' rituals.

This approach to kingship was echoed at Ireland's other royal centres. Navan Fort (page 61), for example, is widely acknowledged as the site of Emain Macha, the ancient capital of Ulster. It featured extensively in the early legends as Conchobar's court and, as a result, there were numerous descriptions of its sumptuous appearance. The palace, it was said, had nine great chambers made of red yew, adorned with bronze pillars and silver ceilings, together with magnificent storehouses, full of fine armour and treasure. When archaeologists investigated the site, however, they found no sign of any military equipment or opulent belongings. Instead, it was clear that Navan Fort had been an important ritual site. At around the time when Conchobar was supposed to have ruled, the main structure was a huge, circular building, supported on thick, wooden posts. It was never used as a residence, but was deliberately burned to the ground, apparently as a form of sacrifice.

Niall of the nine hostages

The various royal lists, which were transmitted by oral means, claimed to trace the high kings back to the twentieth century BC, but in fact it is hard to discern the careers of any genuine Irish rulers, prior to the fourth century AD. Niall of the Nine Hostages is usually cited as the first historical high king. He is said to have reigned from AD 379–405, but this, along with most other details of his rule, is a matter of some debate. Niall is reputed to have earned his impressive nickname by taking hostages from the chiefs of the five ancient provinces, as well as from the Scots, the Britons, the Saxons and the Gauls. In reality, though, he is very unlikely to have wielded this much power and probably took all nine from a local tribe, the Airgialla.

The Stone of Destiny

The Scots retained many elements of the Irish system of kingship, when they migrated from Ulster to Argyll (see page 61). In particular, they may have brought with them a sacred stone, for use in their inauguration rites. Some believe that this was the original *Lia Fáil*, others that it was the celebrated Stone of Destiny. Either way, it was originally sited at Dunadd, before being moved to Scone. This, like Tara, became an important religious site, because it was deemed the geographical centre of Scotland. Here, the authority of the new king was confirmed, not by a coronation (crowning was a later development), but by taking his seat on the Stone of Destiny and receiving the acclamation of his peers.

✹ Grianán of Aileach

COUNTY DONEGAL

This imposing hill-fort was once renowned as the royal capital of Ulster, following the destruction of Emain Macha. Its origins are shrouded in legend. According to tradition, it was built by the ancient gods, the Tuatha Dé Danaan. In some stories, it was described as the home of the Dagda, the father of the gods, while in others it was cited as the burial place of a different Danaan leader, Nuadu of the Silver Arm. Yet another tradition suggests that it belonged to three brothers, Mac Cuill, Mac Cécht and Mac Gréine, who killed Lugh and divided Ireland amongst themselves. In a later tale, Mac Cuill was cited as a pagan king, converted to Christianity by St Patrick. The well where he is believed to have undergone his conversion is shown, left.

In historical terms, the kingdom of Aileach was ruled by a branch of the northern Uí Néill dynasty, after the fortress itself was captured in *c.* 425 AD by Eógan, son of Niall of the Nine Hostages. It was looted in the seventh century by the southern Uí Néill and suffered even greater damage in 1102, when it was largely destroyed by Muirchertach O'Brien, King of Munster. The present structure, although impressive, is somewhat misleading, since it was virtually rebuilt during the restoration of 1874–8.

൭ Mound of the Hostages

TARA **COUNTY MEATH**

Tara was both the most sacred and the most regal place in ancient Ireland. Revered as a ritual site, it was also the seat of the high kings, who claimed supremacy over the entire country. Here, the new kings were chosen and inaugurated by the druids, using a mystical ceremony known as the *tarbhfhess* ('bull-sleep'). They were also expected to participate in a ritual union with the goddess Maeve (see page 43).

In reality, many of the monuments at Tara are pre-Celtic. Annalists acknowledged the antiquity of the site by claiming that its royal links extended back to the twentieth century BC, when Sláinge became the first high king. Conn of the Hundred Battles (second century AD) and Cormac mac Airt (third century AD) featured frequently in the early legends, but the first historical ruler appears to have been Niall of the Nine Hostages (fourth to fifth century). This mound was named after him, although it is actually a Neolithic passage-grave.

✸ Connemara

COUNTY GALWAY

Connemara takes its name from *Conmaicne Mara* ('Conmac's people of the Sea') and refers to the ancient, legendary ruler, who created the first kingdom in this area, although there is disagreement over his precise identity. Some believe that it was Conmac, the illegitimate child of Maeve and Fergus mac Róich. This theory is strengthened by the fact that their other child, Ciar, fulfilled a similar role, becoming the ancestor of the inhabitants of Kerry. The more popular view, however, is that the relevant figure was Lugaid Conmac.

According to the *Cycle of Kings*, Lugaid was a leader of the Erainn tribe, who ruled in the second century AD. He lost his throne at the Battle of Cenn Abrat and was forced to flee to Scotland, accompanied by a handful of loyal retainers. There, he befriended the Scottish king, who helped him to regain his crown. Lugaid also ruled at Tara for a time, before being replaced by his foster-son, Cormac mac Airt.

✸ Rock of Cashel

COUNTY TIPPERARY

Although it is probably best known today for its mythical links with St Patrick, Cashel grew to fame as a royal stronghold, the capital of the kings of Munster. According to legend, it was founded by Corc mac Luigthig, as the result of a vision, in which he saw a yew bush growing out of a boulder. Corc's druids interpreted this as a sign that his descendants would be kings and, indeed, he was later acknowledged as the dynastic ancestor of the Eóganachta (literally 'the people born out of the yew'). Cashel remained a royal centre for more than 500 years, its most celebrated ruler being Brian Boru. Then in 1101, Muirchertach O'Brien presented it to the Church.

꧁ Dunadd Fort

KILMARTIN VALLEY **ARGYLL**

This rocky outcrop holds a special place in the history of the Scottish people, as their first capital on the mainland. Originally, the Scots were a tribe from Ulster. Then in *c.* 500 AD, a group migrated to Argyllshire, where they founded the kingdom of Dalriada. Gradually, they expanded eastwards, largely at the expense of the Picts, until the two kingdoms merged in *c.* 843. At this stage, the capital was transferred away from Dunadd.

While conducting excavations on this site, archaeologists discovered carvings of a boar and a footprint, which may well have played a part in the inauguration rites of early Scottish kings. According to tradition, the Scots also brought across from their Irish homeland a sacred, ritual stone, for use in these royal ceremonials. Many believe this to have been the Stone of Destiny, which was later transferred to Scone, before being carried off to England by Edward I.

꧁ Navan Fort

COUNTY ARMAGH

This Bronze Age hill-fort is generally recognized as the site of Emain Macha, the ancient royal seat of the kings of Ulster. As *Isamnion*, it appeared on Ptolemy's world map (second century AD), and the discovery among the ruins of a Barbary ape's skull – presumably an exotic gift from a visiting dignitary – confirms that the place was well known beyond Ireland's shores. Through the legends, it was famed, above all, as the court of King Conchobar, which contained the fabulous Red Branch palace.

℮℮ Rannoch Moor

PERTHSHIRE

The bleak desolation of Rannoch Moor is probably best known today as the setting for the dramatic chase in Robert Louis Stevenson's *Kidnapped* (1886). The novelist was inspired, however, by the area's long tradition as a haven for outlaws and freedom-fighters. In particular, both William Wallace and Robert the Bruce are thought to have sheltered here, during their struggles against the English.

Wallace's guerrilla activities began in 1297, just a year after Edward I had assumed control of Scotland. The immediate cause was a quarrel with the English Sheriff of Lanark, which resulted in the latter's death. Wallace was outlawed and, within a matter of weeks, had become the leader of a resistance movement. During this period, the wilder haunts of Perthshire were his favourite base. A few years later, Robert the Bruce also took refuge on Rannoch Moor. After crowning himself king in 1306, he was heavily defeated by Edward's troops at the Battle of Methven. His army was scattered and he needed time to rebuild his forces, before resuming the struggle in 1307.

Dunnottar Castle
KINCARDINE

Dunnottar was originally a Pictish fortress, but its royal connections date from a much later era. During the Civil War, it guarded the 'Honours of Scotland' – the crown, sceptre and sword of state. It also housed the private papers of Charles II, who was a guest at the castle. Cromwell's troops laid siege to Dunnottar, hoping to capture these prizes, but both eluded their grasp. The papers were smuggled out by Anne Lindsay, stitched into her clothing, while the royal regalia were moved to a new hiding-place, beneath the pulpit of nearby Kinneff church.

Cawdor Castle
NAIRN

Cawdor Castle has long been associated with Macbeth, the notorious king portrayed in Shakespeare's play. According to the playwright, he was promised the title of Thane of Cawdor on the 'blasted heath', which itself was supposedly located just a few miles away, at Hardmuir. Shakespeare was correct in locating Macbeth's career in this area – his true title was Mormaer of Moray and he was, indeed, the last Scottish king to rule from the Highlands – but his assessment of Macbeth's character was misleading. Far from being a villainous tyrant, he was apparently a popular and successful ruler.

◉ Dumbarton Rock

DUNBARTONSHIRE

This rocky stronghold takes its name from *Dún Breatann* ('Fortress of the Britons'). It rose to prominence as the capital of Strathclyde, a small kingdom in the south-west. These Britons were a Celtic race, who reached the peak of their influence between the fifth and eighth century. They remained independent until 1018, when Malcolm II installed Duncan (the murdered ruler in *Macbeth*) as king of Strathclyde. After this, it rapidly became absorbed into the kingdom of Scotland.

The original fortress at Dumbarton dated back to at least the sixth century, although few traces of this have survived. The Rock retained its strategic importance, however, and its castle was garrisoned until the late eighteenth century. William Wallace may have been held captive here, before being sent to his death in London. There are also links with Mary Queen of Scots, who stayed at the castle in 1548, on her way to France. Dumbarton later became a stronghold for her followers, until its capture in 1571.

∽∂ Brechin Cathedral

ANGUS

Although it was created a royal burgh in 1641, Brechin's chief royal connection dates from an earlier era. For it was here, in July 1296, that John Balliol renounced his crown, presenting both his royal insignia and his realm to Edward I of England. This ignominious episode stemmed from Balliol's disastrous decision to form an alliance with the French and launch an attack on northern England. Edward swiftly crushed the revolt, winning an overwhelming victory at Dunbar in April 1296, before exacting his revenge on the hapless Balliol.

∽∂ Dunkeld Abbey

PERTHSHIRE

Dunkeld rose to prominence during the reign of Kenneth MacAlpin, who is traditionally regarded as the first true king of Scotland. In c. 843, he managed to unite the Picts and the Scots of Dalriada under a single crown. He called this new territory 'Alba', although it was soon to form the nucleus of the kingdom of Scotland. In order to secure his lands, Kenneth chose two new capitals. Forteviot, in the heart of Pictland, became his political stronghold, while Dunkeld was selected as the spiritual capital. As confirmation of this, St Columba's relics were transferred here from Iona.

ᕮᕮ Kilchurn Castle

LOCH AWE **ARGYLL**

Not every Scot supported the Jacobite claim to the Scottish throne. Many of the Campbells remained loyal to King George II during the '45 Rebellion and, indeed, this splendid castle was offered as a garrison for Hanoverian troops. By this stage, Kilchurn had already been a valuable stronghold for more than 300 years, ever since it was built by Sir Colin Campbell of Glenorchy in 1440. Its days were numbered, however, for it was severely damaged in the 1760s, after being struck by lightning.

ᕮᕮ Edinburgh

MIDLOTHIAN

Edinburgh was an important, royal stronghold, long before the nation of Scotland was formed. In the fifth century, it became the capital of the tiny kingdom of Gododdin, which was situated in the Lothians. Its Celtic inhabitants lived a precarious existence in the shadow of the Angles of Bernicia, who eventually captured Edinburgh in 638.

The first Scottish monarchs to live here were probably Malcolm Canmore (ruled 1058–93) and his wife, St Margaret. She died in the castle and her son, David I, built a chapel in her honour, which is one of the oldest surviving parts of the present structure. Mary Queen of Scots was also a resident here, giving birth to her son, James VI, in a tiny room above Grassmarket. Legend has it that the infant was smuggled out of the castle in a basket, lowered from the window. The castle also served as a hiding-place for the Scottish regalia. These were concealed at the time of the Act of Union (1707) and were only 'rediscovered' by Sir Walter Scott in 1818.

HEROES

The majority of the ancient Celtic legends which have come down to us deal with the exploits of heroes. In Ireland, these are contained in two impressive cycles of stories. The first, usually known as the Ulster Cycle, revolves around the heroic deeds of Cú Chulainn. With his superhuman strength, he defends his native land, battling against Maeve and her invading army. The second cycle, which is more romantic in character, deals with the adventures of Finn MacCool and his companions. These tales have often been compared to the legend of King Arthur and the Knights of the Round Table.

Scotland cannot boast of an equivalent store of ancient literature. Instead, its heroes were drawn from the reality of its long struggle for nationhood. This was epitomized by the campaigns which Robert the Bruce and William Wallace waged against the English Crown.

Caerlaverock Castle, Dumfries
A stronghold of the Maxwells, this castle had its finest hour in the siege of 1301, when sixty defenders held out for two days against an English force of 3,000 men.

Heroic legend

Many ancient sites in Ireland carry mythological associations. Of these, most relate to the heroes described in the early legends, rather than to gods or kings, although the dividing line between these different categories is often a very tenuous one.

The oldest and most celebrated group of Irish stories is the Ulster Cycle, which is centred on Cú Chulainn, the great champion of the north. At the heart of this cycle is an epic tale called the *Táin Bó Cuailgne* ('Cattle Raid of Cooley'). In this, Maeve, Queen of Connacht, decides to steal a magical bull from the neighbouring kingdom of Ulster. She feels safe in doing so, because the Ulstermen are stricken by a curse, which prevents them from fighting. One man alone is immune from the spell. This is Cú Chulainn, the supreme warrior-hero, who fights a valiant rearguard action against the Connacht army, until his fellow countrymen have recovered sufficiently to bring about Maeve's defeat.

An age of heroism

The Ulster Cycle appears to date from around the first century BC, providing a vivid portrait of Iron Age society. This was a heroic age, when fighting skills, bravery in the face of death, and personal glory were prized above all other qualities. The popularity of the *Táin* prompted some people to try and identify the sites mentioned in the saga. But, as the action of the story was largely confined to Ulster, the scope of this was limited.

Magic and myth

The second main collection of legends was contained in the Fionn or Fenian Cycle. This was set in a later age, the third century AD, when Cormac mac Airt was the high king at Tara. The mood of these tales is very different from the *Táin*. In place of the latter's enthusiasm for feats of strength and warlike heroism, there is a more courtly atmosphere. Magic plays a greater part, with many of the stories set in enchanted castles or mysterious caves.

Nominally at least, the principal focus of the cycle was Finn MacCool. In fact, he featured in comparatively

Watling Lodge Antonine Wall, Stirling
Built in AD 143–4, the Antonine Wall was the Roman frontier between the Forth and the Clyde. This section was protected by a ditch.

few of the tales, and was often overshadowed by other members of the Fianna, such as Ossian, Diarmaid and Oscar. The diffuse nature of the legends did mean, however, that the sites associated with them were spread over a much greater area of Ireland.

In addition, the Fionn Cycle remained popular with storytellers for a much longer period than the *Táin*. This meant that, over the centuries, the character of the tales was altered. Later versions were often heavily Christianized. The *Acallam na Senórach* ('Colloquy of the Old Men'), for example, described how Ossian survived to meet up with St Patrick. Their conversation took place while they shared a journey and, on the way, the aged warrior reminisced with the holy man about his youthful exploits with the Fianna, pointing out where individual adventures had taken place. This type of story, which linked topography and legend, became extremely popular in the Middle Ages.

In addition to the *Acallam*, there was another anthology of similar material called the *Dindshenchas* ('Lore of Prominent Places'), which was preserved in the *Book of Leinster* (*c.* 1150). Texts of this kind were highly influential in forging a link between places and legends, throughout the Irish countryside.

Legends of Scotland

Scotland did not produce the same, rich corpus of oral legend as Ireland. Indeed, the nearest equivalent is prob-

ably the collection of tales about Fingal, which were concocted in the eighteenth century by James Macpherson, in imitation of the myths about Finn MacCool (see page 79). Instead, the main hero-related sites are drawn from historical figures, such as William Wallace, Robert the Bruce or Bonnie Prince Charlie.

The most famous locations are those linked with genuine battles, such as Stirling (above) or Bannockburn, but all of these figures attracted legends of their own. There are many caves in Scotland, for instance, which purport to be the spot where Robert the Bruce drew inspiration from watching a spider weave its web. Similarly, Blind Harry's epic poem, *Wallace* (*c.* 1477), featured dozens of legends about the Scottish freedom-fighter.

Stirling Castle, Stirling
Two famous victories over the English were won within view of this castle. Wallace defeated them at Stirling Bridge (1297), while Bruce achieved even greater success at Bannockburn (1314).

☉ Giant's Causeway

COUNTY ANTRIM

Giants appear quite frequently in Irish legend, although the use of the term is rather inconsistent. Some characters were permanently large, but the word was also used in connection with numerous warrior-heroes, who were normally portrayed as human. Later versions of the myths relating to Finn, Ossian and Diarmaid, for example, all describe them as giants. Evidently, the term could be employed quite loosely, to signify importance.

In this particular case, the giant is usually interpreted as Finn MacCool (see page 82). Although the tale does not appear in any of the ancient story cycles, there is a longstanding tradition that Finn fell in love with a giantess from the island of Staffa, and built a magical bridge across the water, so that they could be reunited. Several authorities, however, cite the Fomorians as the creators of the Causeway, noting that it is sometimes known in Irish as *Clochan na bhFómharach* ('Stones of the Fomorians'). These creatures were normally portrayed as monstrous demons (see page 41).

Glencoe

ARGYLL

Glencoe is probably better known for its victims than its heroes. In essence, it marked the first of the clashes between Jacobite supporters and the English crown. In 1688, James VII had been deposed, to be replaced by the joint rule of William and Mary. This proved unpopular in the Highlands, where many clansmen regretted the ending of the Stuart line. In order to bolster his authority, William gave orders that the Highland Chiefs should swear an oath of allegiance. The MacDonalds of Glencoe complied, but the papers arrived too late, and so the king decided to make an example of them. Accordingly, on the night of 12 February 1692, a detachment of Campbell troops attacked the MacDonalds, killing at least thirty-eight of them.

A few, individual acts of defiance may well have occurred. Some soldiers are said to have killed domestic animals, in order to bloody their swords and prove their obedience to their officers. Even so, the massacre was widely condemned as an atrocity. As for Glencoe itself, it lived up to its nickname, 'the Valley of Weeping'.

Fingal's Cave

STAFFA

Fingal was essentially the Scottish equivalent of the legendary, Irish hero, Finn MacCool (see page 82). The character was made famous by James Macpherson, who published 'translations' of ancient epics in his *Fingal* (1762) and *Temora* (1763). Although largely concocted by the author himself, these stories proved immensely popular during the Romantic era and inspired the name of this remarkable geological site. The place itself had only recently been discovered (1772) and was much visited by the Romantic glitterati, including Turner and Keats.

◎◎ The Blasket Islands

COUNTY KERRY

This area was home to Cú Roi, the champion of Munster. He was famed for his immense strength and could only be killed by his own sword. For further security, he lived in a stronghold which rotated after dusk, so that no nocturnal attacker could ever find its entrance.

In many ways, Cú Roi was the southern equivalent to Ulster's hero, Cú Chulainn, and the pair featured together in several legends. The most famous of these was a prototype for the Arthurian tale of *Sir Gawain and the Green Knight*. In this, Cú Roi appeared at a feast in disguise, challenging three Ulster heroes to prove their bravery, by striking off his head and then allowing him to return the blow. The first two failed the test, but Cú Chulainn proved his courage by offering his bare neck to the headless stranger. After this, Cú Roi revealed his identity and declared Cú Chulainn the supreme hero.

Valour of a very different kind was required in 1588, when the remains of the defeated Spanish Armada tried to make its way home past Ireland. Already in a ragged state, the ships were buffeted by storms, and two of them – the *Santa Maria de la Rosa* and the *San Juan de Ragusa* – foundered in Blasket Sound.

෨ Eildon Hills

ROXBURGH

Several legends are associated with this romantic spot. Originally, the Eildons formed a single mountain, but Michael Scot, the wizard of the Borders, persuaded a demon to split them into three separate peaks. Here, too, was the home of Thomas of Ercildoune, better known as Thomas the Rhymer. He met with the Queen of the Faeries on these slopes, travelling with her to Fairyland. There, he acquired the gift of divination, which enabled him to produce a celebrated book of prophecies.

෨ Finn MacCool's Finger Stone

EASKY **COUNTY SLIGO**

After Cú Chulainn, Fionn mac Cumhaill or Finn MacCool (the anglicized version) was the most popular character in Irish legend. An entire cycle of stories was devoted to him and to his companions, the Fianna. Indeed, their exploits have often been compared to those of King Arthur and his knights. As a result, many sites in Ireland allude to Finn's career.

The unusual name of this stone refers to one of Finn's best-known legends, even though the digit in question is actually a thumb, rather than a finger. In his youth, Finn went to train under the druid, Finnegas. As part of his duties, he had to prepare food for his mentor and, on one occasion, he was asked to cook a magical creature – the salmon of knowledge. Finnegas told him not to touch the fish, but Finn accidentally burned his thumb on it. In doing so, he gained the power of divination, which was to serve him well in his adventures.

◎◎ Ossian's Grave

GLENAAN **COUNTY ANTRIM**

Oisin, or Ossian, was the son of Finn MacCool and a leading member of his warrior band, the Fianna. His name means 'little deer', in reference to the strange story attached to his birth. Ossian's mother, Sadb, had come under the influence of an evil druid, who transformed her into a fawn. Finn first encountered her when she was in this shape, but he managed to undo the spell and restore her to her former state. After this, the couple fell in love and married. While Sadb was pregnant with Ossian, however, the druid returned and abducted her. Finn searched high and low for seven years and, though he never found Sadb again, he did come across a young boy living wild in the forest. This was the youthful Ossian, who had been raised in the woods by his mother. Finn rejoiced at this discovery, though he mourned the loss of Sadb, who was now trapped forever in the form of a deer.

◎◎ Kilclooney Dolmen

COUNTY DONEGAL

At Kilclooney, there are a pair of portal dolmens, which are popularly known as the 'Beds of Diarmaid and Gráinne'. This unfortunate couple featured in one of Ireland's most poignant love stories. In his later years, Finn MacCool became engaged to Gráinne, the daughter of the high king, but she preferred a young warrior called Diarmaid. The lovers eloped together, but Finn pursued them relentlessly for many years. During their flight, they were obliged to sleep out in the wild, before eventually being rescued by Oenghus, the god of love.

ᐇ Ben Bulben

COUNTY SLIGO

This mysterious mountain featured prominently in the ancient legends, usually as a place of ill omen. It was here that Finn discovered his son, Ossian, after an evil druid had spirited away his mother (see page 84). It was here, too, many years later, that Finn had a fatal encounter with one of his warriors, bringing the tale of Diarmaid and Gráinne to a tragic conclusion (see page 84).

After the couple had been rescued by Oenghus, Finn made a public show of reconciliation with them. Beneath the surface, however, he still harboured a deep resentment against Diarmaid and thirsted for revenge. His opportunity arose when the pair went out hunting together on the slopes of Ben Bulben. During the chase, Diarmaid suffered a terrible wound from an enchanted boar. Finn might have rescued him but he declined, preferring instead to watch his rival die. Inevitably, Finn's reputation was damaged, weakening his leadership of the Fianna.

✹ Dunseverick Castle

COUNTY ANTRIM

The Irish name for this fortress is *Dún Sobhairce*, which featured in a number of ancient legends. The most celebrated of these was *How Ronan Slew his Son*, in which it was identified as the residence of King Eochaid. Out of friendship, the latter offered his daughter in marriage to Ronan, the king of Leinster. Tragedy ensued, however, when the princess fell in love with Ronan's son, Máel Fothartaig. He rejected her and, in revenge, she claimed that he had tried to rape her. In a fury, Ronan had Máel executed, only to die of grief when he learned the truth.

✹ Church Island

COUNTY KERRY

On Church Island, situated near the tiny island of Beginish, there is an early Christian monastic site, shown right. Beginish lies just off the coast of the Ring of Kerry, and here there is an ancient stone with an inscription dedicated to Lir. Appropriately for such a location, Lir was a marine deity and his son, Manannán mac Lir, became the principal sea-god in the Irish pantheon. A powerful figure, he travelled over the waves in either a sea-chariot or a magical curragh, wielding a terrible sword called *Frecraid* ('The Answerer'), which dealt death at every blow.

Lir himself featured less prominently in the early myths, although he may perhaps be linked with the central character in *The Fate of the Children of Lir*. In this famous tale, he was a king whose children were turned into swans by a wicked sorceress. In addition, Lir can probably be identified with the Welsh sea-god, Llyr, who appeared in the *Mabinogion*. More interestingly, perhaps, he may also have provided part of the inspiration for Shakespeare's *King Lear*.

✸ Dun Eóganachta

INISHMORE **COUNTY GALWAY**

This striking fortress was named after a member of
Munster's ruling family. For the Eóganachta were a
historical dynasty, who dominated politics in the South
for hundreds of years (fifth to tenth century), prior to the
rise of Brian Boru.

The origins of the Eóganachta, however, are buried in
the mists of legend. According to some sources, their
founder was Corc mac Luigthig (see page 59). Others,
meanwhile, cite Mug Nuadat as the ancestor. Mug was an
ancient, legendary king, who was said to have reigned
over the entire southern half of Ireland. This mythical
domain was known as *Leth Moga* ('Mug's Half').
Certainly, it was Mug's descendants, who gave the dynasty
its name. More specifically, it came from his grandson
Eógan, who featured in several legends of his own, usually
in contention with his brother, Lugaid Conmac (see page
59). Their rivalry came to a head at the Battle of Cenn
Abrat, where Lugaid was defeated.

✸ Slieve League

COUNTY DONEGAL

This region has strong links with Conall Gulban, one of
the sons of Niall of the Nine Hostages. Its Irish name is
Tir Chonaill (literally 'Conall's Land'). Together with his
brothers, Eógan and Enna, he is thought to have been
responsible for the destruction of Emain Macha (see page
61). Conall is also said to have given his name to Ben
Bulben (originally *Beinn Ghulbain*), after losing his life
there under heroic circumstances. He was attempting to
rescue a Leinster princess from a giant, but was slain in
the process.

✺ Dundalk

COUNTY LOUTH

Dundalk takes its name from its supposed creator, a legendary chieftain called Dealga (the literal meaning is *Dún Dealgan* or 'Dealga's Fort'). He belonged to the Fir Bolg, a shadowy race who ruled Ireland before the Tuatha Dé Danaan. The place was made famous, however, by a later owner of the stronghold. This was Cú Chulainn, the champion of Ulster, who lived in the fort as a boy, before taking it as his own. Cú Chulainn's exploits are recounted in *The Cattle Raid of Cooley* where, almost single-handedly, he defended Ulster from Maeve's army.

✺ Clach MhicLeoid

HARRIS

It was not unusual in Celtic territories for an ancient tomb or monument to be linked with a legendary figure. More uncommon, though, was the notion of naming it after a real person. Situated close to the Sound of Taransay, this prehistoric standing stone was originally designed for astronomical purposes, but it has come to be known by the name of the dominant clan on Harris. The founder of the family was a thirteenth-century Norseman, Leod, who inherited Lewis and Harris, together with part of Skye.

෨ Pictish Stone

ABERLEMNO **ANGUS**

Many Pictish carvings are hard to decipher but, uniquely, this example is thought to be a record of a historical event. For historians believe that the eighth-century stone may commemorate a local conflict, the Battle of Nechtansmere (685), where the Picts won a heroic victory over the Angles. The latter wear helmets with long nose-guards, which are similar to those found in Anglian territory, while the Picts fight bare-headed. At the top, a Pictish horseman pursues an Angle, who has lost his weapon, and the rout is confirmed at the bottom, where an Anglian corpse is picked clean by a crow.

෨ Culloden

INVERNESS

In stark contrast to the above, this is the site of a military catastrophe. After his disastrous attempt to claim the throne, Bonnie Prince Charlie fled back to Scotland, pursued by the English forces. The two armies met at Culloden Moor on 16 April 1746, where the Scots suffered a crushing defeat. The Duke of Cumberland, the English commander, became known as 'the Butcher', after giving orders that all wounded prisoners were to be killed. The Jacobite cause never recovered from this appalling setback.

◎ Eilean Donan Castle

ROSS & CROMARTY

Eilean Donan is probably Scotland's most picturesque castle, appearing as a decorative backdrop in such films as *Highlander* and *The World is not Enough*. Its beauty is misleading, however, for it has also been the scene of many violent conflicts. Built on the site of an Iron Age fort, the present castle was begun by Alexander II, in an attempt to bolster the region's defences against Viking attacks. Later, it passed to the Mackenzies of Kintail, who appointed the MacRaes as Constables of the stronghold.

The Mackenzies were staunch Jacobites and this resulted in the most extraordinary episode in Eilean Donan's history. For in 1719, the chief of the clan launched an abortive uprising, after installing a substantial force of Spanish soldiers in the castle. Hearing of this, the English king sent a party of frigates to root out the rebels. In the course of the fighting, much of the castle was blown up with gunpowder. Eilean Donan remained a ruin until the early twentieth century, when it was extensively restored.

HOLY MEN

The Celts remained a potent force in their western strongholds long into the Christian period. Indeed, in some cases it is possible to trace the conversion process in Scotland and Ireland by following the course of the monasteries and churches, which sprang up in their wake. Celtic Christianity was very different from the organized system preferred by the Papacy. Missionaries, monks and anchorites played a far greater role in spreading the gospel, and physical reminders of their arduous lifestyle can still be seen in many parts of the Celtic landscape.

The missionaries did not shrink from making use of their Celtic heritage, as they carried the Word to the heathens. Influences of the old, pagan styles can often be detected in the manuscripts and liturgical vessels, which were produced for the Church although, in terms of the landscape, it was the ornate, high crosses which created the most lasting effect.

**Bantry Bay,
County Cork**
St Brendan the Navigator (c. 486–c. 575) is said to have embarked from here on the miraculous voyage, which took him to the Land of Promise.

The coming of Christianity

CHRISTIANITY USHERED IN A NEW era in Celtic lands. The Roman Empire had not managed to gather these territories into its fold, but it seemed that the Roman Church might prove more successful in this respect. The first mission to Ireland was not carried out by St Patrick, but by a papal envoy called Palladius, and similar expeditions were despatched to the British mainland. The efforts of Palladius appear to have met with little success, however, and instead it was the Celts themselves who made the crucial, spiritual breakthrough.

St Patrick and St Columba

Two figures, above all, dominated the conversion process: St Patrick and St Columba. Patrick was born in western Britain but, at the age of sixteen, was carried off to Ireland as a slave. After managing to escape, he was determined to return and convert his former masters. His mission probably occurred in c. 450, although this date and the extent of the saint's success have been the subject of much debate.

St Columba preached in the following century, when the conversion of Ireland had largely been completed. As a result, he channelled his efforts towards Scotland, converting Brude, the Pictish king, and consecrating Aidan of Dalriada. More importantly, perhaps, he founded the monastery of Iona, which became the chief base of Celtic Christianity. For Iona developed into the head of a large network of monasteries, both in Scotland and Ireland, which followed the liturgical principles that Columba had laid down.

Monasterboice County Louth Founded by St Buithe, Monasterboice is famed for the beauty of its high crosses. The finest of these was donated by Abbot Muiredach (d. 923).

Growth of the monasteries

Monasticism played a key part in the success of Celtic Christianity. The comparative failure of the Roman missions has often been ascribed to the lack of large urban centres, which were present elsewhere in Europe. Monasteries, on the other hand, could take root in small communities and then expand, if there was sufficient demand. Indeed, monasteries such as Clonmacnois grew to such a size that they assumed the proportions of a small town.

At the other end of the scale, some communities remained tiny, perhaps consisting of an anchorite and a few companions. As these hermits often chose to live in remote and inaccessible spots, evidence of their way of life has often survived. In particular, the bleak remains on the Skellig Islands (pages 104–5) demonstrate the hardships which these converts were willing to endure in order to demonstrate the strength of their faith.

The Celtic missionaries also prospered due to their willingness to compromise. Shrewdly, the early Christians did not demand the closure of all the ancient shrines, preferring to adapt them for their own purposes. It can have been no accident, for example, that St Patrick chose to found his principal church at Armagh (originally Ard Macha), barely a stone's throw away from the important ritual centre of Emain Macha.

Equally, the Celts found no difficulty in adapting their own pagan designs for use on Christian artefacts. The

Ruthwell Cross, Dumfries
Dating from the early eighth century, Ruthwell's cross is a masterpiece of Anglian sculpture, decorated with grotesque beasts and runic inscriptions.

strange beasts at the foot of Monasterboice Cross (opposite), for instance, would have looked perfectly at home on an ancient idol. Initially, the Celts used this type of design on their chalices, their illuminated manuscripts and their shrines, but these opulent objects proved both too tempting and portable when the Vikings began making their raids. So instead, it was their marvellous stone crosses which created the greatest impact. The earliest examples of these resembled ancient standing stones, adorned with a few Christian symbols, but within a century or so this medium had been transformed. The great high crosses represented a final flourish of the Celts' unique style, before both their people and their culture were absorbed into the mainstream of European affairs.

⊚ Loch Maree

ROSS & CROMARTY

Local tradition insists that this popular beauty-spot took its name from St Maelrubba (*c.* 642–*c.* 722), who is thought to have lived as a hermit on one of the islands in the lake. Also known as Malrubius or Maree, the saint originated from Ireland and trained as a monk at Bangor in County Down. Arriving in Scotland, he founded a monastery at Applecross (673), which became one of the most important teaching centres in Scotland, before it was destroyed in a Viking raid.

Maelrubba was not content to remain at Applecross, but continued his missionary work in the area around Loch Broom and on the island of Skye. There, a church named Cill Chriosd marks the site of his cell. Eventually, he was killed by Norsemen and his body was returned for burial, either at Applecross or on the Isle of Maree. At the latter, there was an ancient well associated with the saint, which for many years was thought to have healing powers.

⊚ Garvellach Islands

ARGYLL

The Garvellachs are a small chain of islands, situated at the mouth of the Firth of Lorne. They were a favourite retreat for early Christian converts, who built their own beehive huts and settled here. Remains of a chapel and a graveyard can still be seen, alongside the ruined huts. Little is known about the history of this community but, according to local tradition, it was visited by both St Brendan and St Columba. Indeed, it may be identified with the retreat called 'Hinba', where Columba used to retire periodically for solitary meditation.

◎ The Skelligs

COUNTY KERRY

The Skelligs, a group of rocky islands located off the Ivereagh peninsula, offer a spectacular insight into the way that early anchorites chose to live. The largest of the islands is known as Skellig Michael (left), because of its links with the cult of St Michael. This saint was traditionally associated with lofty places, such as St Michael's Mount and Mont St Michel. The Skelligs have even closer links, however, with another holy man. This is St Finan, who is thought to have established the original settlement on the islands.

Because of their isolated position, the Skelligs have preserved substantial remains of many of these early buildings. There are six *clocháns* (large beehive huts), two small oratories similar to that at Gallarus (page 108), and a flight of 670 steps, hewn out of the rock.

❨❨ Dursey Island

COUNTY CORK

The western shores of Ireland are littered with scores of tiny islands. Dursey, which lies off the coast of the Ring of Beara, is typical of these, having sacred associations for Christian and pagan Celts alike. For Christians, the island was an ideal place to come and live the solitary life – it was removed from the distractions of the secular world, but not too distant from it, should some emergency arise. Here can be seen the early Christian monastery of St Mary's Abbey.

For pagan Celts, Dursey Island had associations with the Otherworld. More specifically, it was believed that the narrow stretch of water between the tip of the Beara peninsula and Dursey concealed the entrance to *Tech Duinn* ('Donn's House'), the Realm of the Dead. Donn was the Irish god of the dead, bearing some similarities to the Roman deity Dis Pater. He was described as a solitary character, preferring to live away from the other deities, surrounded by the souls of the departed. Some Christian commentators linked him with the devil, arguing that *Tech Duinn* was just another name for Purgatory.

◎◎ Gallarus Oratory

COUNTY KERRY

This famous structure provides a fascinating insight into the type of church used by early Christian worshippers. Resembling an upturned boat, it features a drystone building technique, which had scarcely changed since Neolithic times. Apart from the entrance, the only other aperture is a tiny window in the east wall, carved out of a single slab of stone. Nearby, there are several pillar-stones bearing Christian symbols, as well as an inscription dedicated to someone called Colum. Historians have been reluctant to date the oratory, but it is probably contemporary with the many beehive huts in the area.

◎◎ Clonmacnois

COUNTY OFFALY

One of the greatest monasteries in Ireland, Clonmacnois was founded in 545 by St Ciarán. He died within months of its creation and could never have imagined that, at its peak, it would contain no fewer than nine churches. Today, the ruins at Clonmacnois are notable mainly for the splendour of their high crosses and carved gravestones but, in its prime, Clonmacnois was the most important artistic centre in Ireland. Among other things, the *Book of the Dun Cow* and the *Annals of Tigernach* were produced in its scriptorium.

Even so, the round tower at the edge of the graveyard is a telling reminder of the precarious existence, which many early Christian communities were forced to endure. During the period of the Viking raids, towers of this kind were used as places of refuge, sheltering both the treasures of the monastery and the monks themselves. For reasons of security, the entrance to the tower lay six feet above ground-level and could only be reached by a ladder, which was lifted inside in times of emergency.

✸ Glendalough

COUNTY WICKLOW

With its beautiful lakeside setting, Glendalough is probably Ireland's most picturesque monastery. The original settlement was founded by St Kevin (d. 619?), a Leinster prince who gave up the secular life to become a hermit. Despite his desire for isolation, disciples gathered around him and Glendalough grew into a major monastic centre. St Kevin himself became the focus of a series of legends, many of them reflecting his love of nature. The most charming one relates how a blackbird laid an egg in his outstretched hand, after which the saint refused to move until it had hatched out.

✸ White Island

COUNTY FERMANAGH

The Lough Erne region produced a unique form of religious art. Here, pagan influences survived far longer than in other parts of Ireland, inspiring the very strange carvings at Killadeas, Boa Island (see pages 35 and 41) and White Island. At first glance, these mysterious, bug-eyed figures resemble pagan idols, but closer examination of their accessories reveals unmistakable Christian imagery. The second figure from the left, for example, is holding a bell and crozier, both of which are traditional attributes for Irish saints.

✆ Doorty Cross

KILFENORA **COUNTY CLARE**

If an Irish town has the prefix 'Kil-', this often suggests that its origins are ecclesiastical. For, in many cases, it derives from the *cill* or 'cell', in which a hermit made his home. Kilfenora, for example, took its name from *Cill Fhionnabair* ('Finbar's Cell'), but developed from these small beginnings into a bishop's see. Today, it is known mainly for the enigmatic carvings on its high cross. This side, for instance, depicts a bishop with two clerics, attacking a monstrous bird with their croziers.

✆ Saul

COUNTY DOWN

According to tradition, this is close to the spot where St Patrick landed at the start of his mission to convert the Irish. Here, he was given a barn by the local lord, Dichu, to serve as his first church, before proceeding to establish his main base at Armagh. Saul takes its name from this *sabhal* or 'barn', and an Augustinian monastery was later founded on the site. Patrick is also said to have died in Saul, although several other locations in Ireland have also claimed this distinction.

Dysert O'Dea

COUNTY CLARE

The spread of Christianity in Ireland owed much to the strength of the anchoretic movement – the desire of some converts to become 'exiles for Christ'. This was often reflected in local place-names. Dysert O'Dea, for example, was originally known as Dísert Tola. A *dísert* ('desert') was a popular name for a hermitage, while St Tola (d. 737) founded a nearby church. He is portrayed as a bishop on Dysert's high cross, and his crozier and bell are preserved at the National Museum in Dublin.

Pillar-Stone

GLENCOLUMBKILLE **COUNTY DONEGAL**

This picturesque valley takes its name from St Columba, who is said to have confronted a group of demons here. In memory of this, an unusual form of pilgrimage was introduced. Before sunrise on the saint's feast day, worshippers are expected to complete a three-mile circuit in the area, visiting fifteen separate 'stations'. Most of these are slabs or pillar-stones, adorned with elaborate carvings, although the tour also includes some prehistoric sites and rock formations, such as Columcille's Chair.

෨ Hill of Slane

COUNTY MEATH

According to tradition, this is the place where St Patrick first threw down the gauntlet to the forces of paganism. At the start of a heathen fire festival, when all flames were supposed to be extinguished and then re-lit from the sacred hearth at Tara, Patrick built a bonfire of his own, to celebrate Easter. This led to a direct confrontation with the high king, Laoghaire, and – so the legend goes – a contest of magical skills with his druids. Patrick emerged victorious, symbolizing the triumph of Christianity.

෨ Christian Pillar-Stones

CARNDONAGH   **COUNTY DONEGAL**

The evolution of the Celtic high cross was a very gradual process. Initially, Christian artists simply added their decorations to existing standing stones, before developing the free-standing cross. Carndonagh's monuments, dating from as early as the seventh century, illustrate the start of this process. The central pillar has a rough cruciform shape, but the flanking stones are straightforward slabs. Similarly, the designs still bear the influence of the pagan Celtic style. The human figures, in particular, are heavily stylized and are reminiscent of the Boa Island carvings.

☙ Durrow Cross

COUNTY OFFALY

This illustrates the Irish high cross at the peak of its development. The cross is combined with a wheel, which may originally have been meant to represent a halo, or else was simply an adaptation of an older sun symbol. The idea was probably borrowed from the processional crosses, which were used in some church services. At the top of the cross, there is a box-like shape, resembling a miniature house with sloping roofs. This was inspired by a type of reliquary, which was very popular with the Celts.

The cross itself is covered in miniature scenes, taken from the Scriptures. These served a practical purpose, since outdoor sermons were often conducted beside the high cross. Accordingly, the images provided a similar, educational function to those on stained-glass windows. At the centre of the cross, there was usually a depiction of the Crucifixion on one side and, as here, a Last Judgement on the other. All the scenes were linked together by flowing spirals and knotwork designs, which were ultimately derived from pagan Celtic metalwork.

☙ Moone Cross

NEAR BALLITORE **COUNTY KILDARE**

As the format of the high cross developed, its illustrations became more naturalistic and sophisticated, echoing the way that the Celtic Church was increasingly absorbed into mainstream Christianity. The images at Moone, however, provide a delightful exception to the rule. The childlike stylization of the figures are much truer to the spirit of ancient Celtic art, and have made the cross far more appealing to modern eyes. This particular scene illustrates the Flight into Egypt.

Moone belonged to the Columban network of monasteries and the high cross was dedicated to St Columba himself. It probably dates from the ninth century.

⊚ Iona Abbey

IONA

Forever linked with the name of St Columba (*c*. 521–97), this is rightly regarded as Scotland's most sacred shrine. The saint's early career was spent in his native Ireland, but in 563 he arrived here with twelve companions, having been granted land for a monastery by the ruler of Dalriada. From this base, Columba sent out missions which carried the gospel to many parts of the Scottish mainland and islands. As part of this conversion process, other monastic communities were created, both in Scotland and Ireland. All of these followed the practices which had been established at Iona, making the Columban federation of monasteries the dominant force in Celtic Christianity. In order to help spread the word, Iona set up a flourishing workshop, where many holy manuscripts were produced including, almost certainly, the celebrated *Book of Kells*.

Iona's later history was more troubled. Successive Viking attacks forced the monks to transfer their most precious possessions to Kells (see page 123). The island also suffered badly during the Reformation, when all but three of its 360 crosses were pulled down. The present abbey was heavily restored in the twentieth century.

⊚ Whithorn Priory

WIGTOWNSHIRE

Whithorn takes its name from the White House (*Huit Aern* in Anglo-Saxon), where St Ninian began his missionary work in *c*. 397. Although there are some doubts about this date, Ninian was certainly the most important of the early missionaries, who sought to evangelize the southern Picts, and this place is rightly known as the cradle of Scottish Christianity. As such, Whithorn remained an important pilgrimage centre until the Reformation. Both Robert the Bruce and Mary Queen of Scots made royal pilgrimages to St Ninian's shrine.

⊚⊙ Strongbow's Tomb

CHRISTCHURCH CATHEDRAL **DUBLIN**

The first Christchurch Cathedral was built in *c.* 1038. Its founder was the Viking king of Dublin, though its bishop, Dunan, was Irish. This church was entirely rebuilt in 1173, and the present building was much restored in the nineteenth century.

Richard de Clare (d. 1176), better known by his nickname 'Strongbow', was the most successful of the Anglo-Norman adventurers, who came to seek their fortune in Ireland. Originally from Wales, he secured his reputation after capturing both Dublin and Waterford. Although he is usually associated with secular affairs, he did commission the rebuilding of the cathedral in 1173.

⊚⊙ Kells Cross

COUNTY MEATH

Few places have played a more significant role in promoting the Celtic, spiritual ideal than Kells. Its early development is uncertain. A monastery may have existed here from as early as the sixth century, and there are theories that this, in turn, was founded on the site of an Iron Age fort. The true importance of the place, however, dates from the early ninth century, when it was chosen as the new headquarters of the Columban network. By this stage, Iona was proving too vulnerable to Viking attacks,

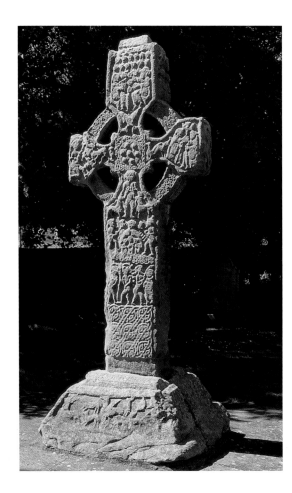

and the relics of St Columba were transferred to Kells. The monastery has lent its name to the *Book of Kells*, even though this was probably produced on Iona. Instead, the most visible signs of its former status are the four high crosses, which have survived to this day.

GLOSSARY

Book of Invasions Anthology of legends relating to ancient invaders.

Boru, Brian The greatest of the Irish high kings (c. 1014).

Broch Circular drystone tower, used as a fortified dwelling.

Cashel Prehistoric stone fort.

Crannog Fortified dwelling, constructed on an artificial island.

Cú Chulainn Legendary Irish warrior, the champion of Ulster.

Cup-mark Cup-shaped hollow, carved into a stone; often encircled by a carved ring, hence the term cup-and-ring mark.

Dalriada First colony founded in Scotland by the ancient Scots; there was also a Dalriada in Ireland.

Dolmen Properly, a portal dolmen; a prehistoric chamber tomb.

Druids Celtic priests, who also acted as judges and royal advisers.

Drystone Built from stone without using mortar.

Fianna Legendary Irish warrior-band, often likened to the Arthurian knights.

Fir Bolg Mythical invaders of Ireland, sometimes identified with the Belgae tribe.

Fomorian A race of deformed demons and pirates.

Henge Stone circle with surrounding earthworks; henges carried ritual overtones and often contained burial sites.

Jacobite A supporter of James VII (James II of England) and his descendants, and the Stuart cause in general.

Mabinogion Early collection of Welsh mythological tales.

Mag Tuired Site of two battles won by the Tuatha Dé Danaan, one over the

	Fir Bolg and the other over the Fomorians.
Midden	Refuse heap in a prehistoric settlement.
Mormaer	A Scottish title, literally a 'high steward'.
Ogham	Rudimentary form of script, employed by the druids.
Otherworld	A supernatural realm, linked to Celtic concepts of the afterlife.
Peel tower	Fortified tower-house, usually entered on the first floor via a ladder; particularly common in the Borders.
Picts	Literally 'the painted ones'; an early Celtic people, mainly based in Scotland.
Quern	A stone for grinding cereal or seeds; often concave and sometimes used in conjunction with a rubbing stone.

Runes	Angular script, carved onto stone or wood; widely used by the Vikings.
Sídhe	Fairy mounds, regarded as the dwelling-places of the Irish gods.
Stone of Destiny	The coronation stone of the Scots, also known as the Stone of Scone.
Táin Bó Cuailgne	The 'Cattle Raid of Cooley'. A famous epic in early Irish literature, in which Cú Chulainn protected Ulster from supernatural foes.
Tuatha Dé Danaan	The ancient gods of Ireland.
Vitrified fort	Prehistoric stone fort with walls that have turned to a glassy mass, after subjection to intense heat; most common in Pictish territory.
Wheelhouse	Iron Age house with partition walls that project inwards, like the spokes of a wheel.

INDEX

ACKNOWLEDGEMENTS

I would like to dedicate this book to Petrina Beaufoy Helm. I owe a great debt of gratitude to her for her patience, her unstinting support and for occasionally getting my name right. Thanks must also go to the terrible twins, Lottie and Lucy, for throwing such wonderful parties.